UPDATED OMAN TRAVEL GUIDE

2024

Discover The Jewel Of The Arabian Peninsula: Your Ultimate Oman Travel Companion.

BY

Robert C. Patricia

Copyright

Table Of Contents

INTRODUCTION

A land with breathtaking landscapes that unfurl like living tapestries, ancient traditions that coexist peacefully with modern marvels, and hospitable people who will make a lasting impression on your soul can be found deep within the Arabian Peninsula. Welcome to Oman, a mesmerizing land of unending natural beauty, vast wilderness, and rich cultural heritage. You will learn with each step you take on this enthralling adventure that Oman is more than just a place to go; it is an emotional journey that will inspire you and forever alter the way you view the world.

You will be mesmerized by the magnificent beauties of Oman as the sun rises above the untamed Al Hajar Mountains, casting a golden glow upon the terracotta settlements nestled within its embrace. Here, the best of the past coexists with cutting-edge innovation to weave a tapestry of contrasts that will astound you. Every region of Oman has a unique tale to tell, begging you to become a part of it. From the busy streets of Muscat, where the fragrant allure of frankincense lingers in the air, to the serene tranquillity of the Wahiba Sands, where sand dunes dance like waves on an ocean of gold.

The complex tapestry of cultures that weaves together the rich fabric of Omani life will leave you breathless in addition to the breathtaking landscapes. The Omani people will welcome you with open arms and a deep respect for tradition because of their real friendliness. Their past includes maritime history, Bedouin heritage, pearl diving, the frankincense trade, and the existence of both modern bazaars and historic souks. You'll come to understand that you are not just a traveler, but an explorer of hearts and souls as you stroll the ancient alleyways, listen to the echoes of ancient tales spoken by the wind, and immerse yourself in the rhythms of Omani life.

As you appreciate the delicious flavors of Omani cuisine, let your taste buds dance with joy. Omani cuisine is a feast of flavors that will awaken your senses, from juicy shuwa that has been slowly cooked in the sands of time to the fragrant blend of spices that embellish every dish. When you eat with locals, you'll discover that the real spirit of Oman isn't just in the food, but also in the relationships that are created over it. In Oman, eating together is a joyous occasion to celebrate life and the benefits of community.

You will be humbled by the size of nature's creations as you explore the untamed wilderness of Jebel Shams, the "Mountain of the Sun," or the magical wadis, hidden oases of green splendour. You will find a haven for the soul in the magnificence of Oman's natural beauties, a place where time stands still and all of your troubles vanish. Oman will embrace you and show you all of its various sides, whether you're an eager adventurer looking for adrenaline-fueled escapades or a thoughtful person wishing for moments of peace.

Beyond the breathtaking scenery and friendly locals, Oman's true character lies in its capacity to arouse emotions and inspire amazement in every visitor. It is an experience that goes beyond the confines of space and time, resonating with the soul long after you say goodbye. Your desire to explore the world, appreciate culture, and protect the marvels that have touched your heart will all be stoked by Oman.

So, dear traveler, embark on this amazing voyage to Arabia's heart. Remember that the true magic of this journey lies not only in the destinations but also in the moments you share, the stories you hear, and the emotions that will weave themselves into your very being.

As you set out on a journey that will touch your spirit and change you for the rest of your life, inhale the aromas of frankincense and adventure, walk softly on the sands of time, and let your heart serve as your compass.

CHAPTER ONE

1.1 Why Visit Oman?

Oman is a fascinating gem in the Arabian Peninsula that is just begging to be discovered. This magical nation, which is nestled between the Arabian Sea and the immense desert landscapes, offers a variety of reasons why it ought to be on every traveler's bucket list.

Rich Cultural legacy: Oman has a long and rich past, with a rich cultural legacy. The nation is a treasure trove of historical delights, from its well-preserved old forts and castles to its traditional souks (markets), where you may immerse yourself in the local culture.

Breathtaking scenery: Oman has a variety of breathtaking scenery. The country's natural beauty is just magnificent, ranging from the majestic Hajar Mountains with its rough peaks and terraced towns to the seemingly infinite golden sand dunes of the Wahiba Sands desert.

Warm Hospitality: The Omani people are well known for their friendly disposition and warm hospitality. You'll be greeted with open arms as you travel the nation, enhancing the experience.

Beautiful Beaches: Oman has a 1,700-kilometer-long coastline that is home to gorgeous beaches and crystal-clear waters. There is a place for every beach lover to relax, from the quiet coves of Musandam to the lively beach scenes in Muscat.

Unusual Wildlife: Oman offers wildlife enthusiasts the chance to see uncommon and exotic animals. Dolphins, whales, and sea turtles can be seen in the surrounding waters, and Arabian oryx and gazelles can be found in the desert regions.

Opportunities for Adventure: There are several chances for thrill-seekers to partake in adventurous activities. Oman provides thrilling adventures, such as dune bashing and camel trekking in the desert and mountain climbing and trekking in the Hajar Mountains.

A delectable variety of flavors can be found in Omani cuisine, which is a delicious combination of Middle Eastern and Indian influences. Try the classic Omani shuwa, a slow-cooked lamb dish, as well as the cool date-based desserts.

Oman is among the Middle East's safest nations to visit in terms of security and stability. It is the perfect destination for both single tourists and families due to its political stability and low crime rates.

Snorkeling and diving: Oman's waters are a diving and snorkeling enthusiast's dream come true. Explore colorful coral reefs and marine life in the Daymaniyat Islands and Muscat's Dimaniyat Islands.

Visits to Oman provide you the opportunity to explore the historic Bedouin culture and learn about customs like falconry and falaj irrigation systems.

Modern Infrastructure: Oman maintains its cultural history but also has state-of-the-art infrastructure that is welcoming and practical for visitors.

In conclusion, Oman provides a seductive fusion of culture, history, the outdoors, and adventure. Oman will capture your heart and leave you with lifelong memories of an extraordinary travel experience, whether you're looking for relaxation on pristine beaches, a cultural tour through historic forts, or exciting escapades in the desert.

1.2 Oman At a Glance

Oman, a fascinating nation on the Arabian Peninsula's southeast coast, is a region of contrasts where old traditions and contemporary advancements coexist together. Oman immediately stands out as a fascinating location that appeals to a wide variety of interests.

Geographical diversity abounds in Oman, which has a combination of craggy mountains, sweeping deserts, and unspoiled coastlines along the Arabian Sea. The northern region is dominated by the high peaks of the Hajar Mountains, while the southern area is home to the Rub' al Khali, the world's biggest continuous sand desert, which is breathtakingly beautiful.

Rich History: Oman has a long, illustrious history that dates back thousands of years. It previously held sway over the maritime world and served as the epicenter of the frankincense trade. The numerous well-preserved old forts, castles, and watchtowers that dot the terrain are proof of this historical significance. The UNESCO-listed Bahla Fort, Nizwa Fort, and Nakhal Fort are among of the most well-known sites.

Cultural Heritage: Tradition and hospitality are ingrained strongly in Omani culture. Oman's citizens take great pride in upholding their traditions and culture. By visiting traditional souks (markets), taking in lively folk dance performances, and participating in cultural festivities like the Muscat Festival, tourists may fully experience the local way of life.

contemporary Progress: Oman has embraced contemporary progress while simultaneously preserving its traditional legacy. The capital city of Muscat is the ideal illustration of this fusion of heritage and modernity. Visitors will discover a blend of contemporary buildings, opulent hotels, and top-notch amenities in this location, which nonetheless has its distinctive Omani flavor.

Spectacular Coastline: The 1,700-kilometer-long coastline of Oman is lined with lovely beaches, fishing communities, and towering cliffs. Numerous chances exist along the shore for water sports like diving, dolphin watching, and snorkeling.

Oman is a wonderland for outdoor enthusiasts who love adventure and nature. Adventurers can partake in pursuits like dune bashing in the Wahiba Sands, mountain hiking, and desert camping beneath the stars. The opportunity to see migratory birds, green turtles, and Arabian oryx will appeal to nature enthusiasts.

Omani Cuisine: This delicious combination of Indian and Middle Eastern cuisines uses a variety of fresh ingredients and aromatic spices. Traditional Omani fare like shuwa, majboos, and halwa provide a fascinating culinary tour.

Overall, Oman's appeal stems from its capacity to meet the needs of every visitor. Whatever your interests—history, environment, culture, or adventure—Oman's allure will leave a lasting impression on your heart and spirit.

1.3 Travel Tips And Etiquette

Traveling to Oman is a rewarding experience that enables you to explore a country with rich traditions and welcoming people. It's crucial to understand the distinctive cultural customs of Oman and abide by these travel advice and etiquette rules to make the most of your visit:

Oman is a conservative Muslim nation with firmly ingrained cultural traditions. Respecting regional traditions and customs is essential. Dress modestly by covering your knees and shoulders, especially in public places. Women may want to cover their hair with a scarf and should think about dressing loosely.

Greetings are an important aspect of Omani culture. Use the traditional salutation "As-salamu alaykum" (peace be upon you) when speaking to locals, and then follow it up with "Wa alaykumu as-salam" (and upon you, peace). Warm handshakes are customary, but you should wait till a woman extends her hand before shaking hers because some women might prefer not to.

Public Shows of Affection: In Oman, public shows of affection are not considered appropriate. To avoid offending others, refrain from hugging, kissing, or holding hands in public.

Ramadan: If you intend to travel during this holy month, keep in mind the customs that are upheld. Respect individuals who are fasting by refraining from eating, drinking, or smoking in public during the day.

When photographing individuals, especially ladies and sacred sites, always get their consent. There are some locations, such as military sites, where photography is prohibited.

Although English is commonly spoken, Arabic is the official language. This is especially true in urban areas and popular tourist spots. The locals will appreciate you for learning a few Arabic greetings like "Marhaba" (hello) and "Shukran" (thank you).

Friday is a Muslim holy day, hence many establishments may be closed during the day, especially for Friday prayers. Consider the religious importance of this day when making your plans.

Tipping: Although it is not customary in Oman, tipping has becoming more popular in tourist destinations. If you thought the service was extraordinary, please consider leaving a little tip.

Alcohol: Alcohol use in public places is not permitted in Oman because of Islamic law. For non-Muslim guests, it is nevertheless offered in authorized hotels and eateries.

Health Warnings: Oman's summers can be particularly hot and humid. Keep yourself hydrated, put on sunscreen, and dress for the weather. Additionally, drinking bottled water instead of tap water is advised.

Negotiating: In Omani markets and souks, haggling is frequent. Price haggling is OK as long as it is done politely and with a smile.

You'll not only respect Oman's culture by following these travel advice and local customs, but you'll also make your trip across this lovely and hospitable nation more fun and meaningful.

CHAPTER TWO

Planning Your Trip

2.1 Best Time To Visit Oman

Oman, a gem of the Arabian Peninsula, is known for its hospitable people, breathtaking scenery, and rich cultural history. Considering the wide variety of attractions and activities available, the optimal time to visit this magical nation might have a significant impact on your trip. Every month in Oman, from January to December, has something special to offer tourists, addressing a range of interests and preferences.

The winter season in Oman, from January to March, is typically regarded as the ideal time to travel there. With nice daytime temperatures between 20°C and 30°C, the climate is perfect for visiting the nation's numerous attractions. Visitors can savor Oman's breathtaking natural splendor, which includes the towering Jebel Akhdar mountains and the wide Wahiba Sands desert. Additionally, because of the pleasant water temperatures and high visibility in coastal regions like Muscat and Salalah, this time of year is ideal for divers.

April to May: Oman undergoes a stunning transition when spring arrives, with landscapes decorated with brilliant flowers and lush foliage. With temperatures ranging from 25°C to 35°C, April and May have a great climate, making them perfect for outdoor pursuits like hiking and exploring historic sites like the Bahla Fort or Nakhal Fort. In addition, during these months, the Salalah region, which is in southern Oman, enjoys the Khareef season, when the monsoon brings mild, foggy weather that transforms the territory into a delightful oasis.

June to August: Oman's summers can be very hot, with highs of 40°C and more. While sea breezes from the shore provide some relief, the heat in the interior may be oppressive. But if you can stand the heat, this is the time to get good hotel deals, especially in Muscat. The annual Muscat Festival, a celebration of Omani culture, heritage, and entertainment, is also the ideal occasion to attend.

September through October: As summer starts to wind down, the months of September and October provide a transitional phase with temperatures that range from 30°C to 35°C. The wadis (dry riverbeds) in Oman are ideal at this time to be explored because they may still contain some water from the previous season's rains. Jebel Shams, Oman's tallest peak, is a well-liked vacation spot at this time of year because of the pleasant weather and breathtaking scenery.

November through December: With temperatures in the range of 25°C to 30°C, November and December are also wonderful months to travel to Oman. The tourist season officially begins during this time, and there are lots of festivals and cultural events happening. The annual Omani National Day events, which highlight the nation's traditions and history, are an immersive experience for tourists.

The best time to visit Oman will depend on your preferences for the weather and the experiences you want to have, in other words. Every month of the year in Oman offers something unique, whether you wish to take advantage of the lovely weather, experience the Khareef season, or take part in cultural events. Plan your vacation appropriately to take full advantage of this enchanting location's distinctive characteristics.

2.2 Visa and Entry Requirements

Oman, an intriguing location with a rich history, breathtaking scenery, and welcoming locals, is found on the Arabian Peninsula's southeast coast. Understanding the visa and entry formalities for this lovely country is crucial before making travel arrangements there.

Visa Waivers: Oman grants visa waivers to nationals of a number of nations for a variety of reasons, including travel, business, and family visits. Oman does not require a visa for citizens of the Gulf Cooperation Council (GCC) nations of Bahrain, Kuwait, Qatar, Saudi Arabia, and the United Arab Emirates. Additionally, visitors from a select group of nations, including the United States, the United Kingdom, Canada, Australia, and the majority of the members of the European Union, can get a visa on arrival for a brief stay.

Citizens of nations not eligible for visa-free entry may apply for an electronic visa, or eVisa, which streamlines the visa application procedure. Depending on the traveler's nationality and purpose of visit, the eVisa can be obtained on the official website of the Royal Oman Police and allows for various sorts of stays, ranging from a few days to a month or more.

Sponsorship: Travelers may occasionally require a sponsor, such as a business or a resident of Oman, to submit a visa application on their behalf. This is typically necessary for extended stays, job applications, and family reunions.

Visitor Permits: Oman provides visitor permits to visitors arriving by sea on cruise ships, enabling them to tour particular defined regions for a set amount of time when the ship is parked in Omani ports. Access to the rest of the nation is not made possible by this permit.

Border Crossings: Oman has a number of border crossings with its neighbors, and the conditions for admission may change based on the checkpoint and the nationality of the visitor. Before organizing an overland trip, it is crucial to verify the most recent information and any relevant travel limitations.

Validity of Passports: It is crucial for all visitors to make sure their passports are valid for at least six months after the day they intend to depart from Oman.

Oman has stringent customs laws, which include limitations on some drugs, alcohol, and forbidden products. To prevent any problems at the crossing, it is advisable to familiarize yourself with the customs regulations.

Travelers can guarantee a simple and enjoyable journey to Oman by being informed of the visa and entry procedures. Before making travel plans, it is best to confirm the most recent information with the Omani embassy or consulate in your home country to be informed of any changes to the laws.

2.3 Choosing The Right Itinerary

To get the most out of your trip to this fascinating Middle Eastern nation, choosing the ideal schedule for your Oman tour is crucial. Oman offers a wide range of experiences that may be customized to your preferences and interests thanks to its rich history, varied landscapes, and cultural treasures. Here are some ideas to help you plan a trip to Oman that you won't soon forget.

Research and Prioritize: Start by learning about Oman's top destinations, events, and activities. Make a list of places you must visit, including the Grand Mosque in Muscat, the Nizwa Fort, Wahiba Sands, Wadi Shab, and Salalah's breathtaking coastline. Organize your travel priorities according to your interests, whether they be in history, nature, adventure, or relaxation.

Oman is a huge country with a variety of scenery, so carefully decide how long you want to stay there. You can visit both the northern and southern regions if you have a week or more to spare. In order to avoid speeding through the experience on a shorter vacation, concentrate on a particular location.

Blend Cultural and Natural Experiences: Oman has a remarkable combination of ancient tradition and stunning scenery. Make sure your schedule includes stops at historical sites, local marketplaces, and cultural icons in addition to wadi, desert, and mountain exploration.

Be sure to provide for travel time because Oman's attractions are dispersed around the country. To make the most of your time and take pleasure in beautiful country drives, think about mixing flights and road vacations.

Incorporate genuine local experiences into your agenda by looking for local experiences. Visit traditional villages, eat at a nearby restaurant, or spend the night in a desert camp under the stars. Your journey will be more rich and interesting if you interact with the local culture.

Plan Your Outdoor Activities: Oman provides a variety of outdoor pursuits, including hiking, scuba diving, and viewing dolphins. Include these activities in your schedule if you enjoy taking on new challenges to spice up your travels.

Consider the Seasons: Oman has warm summers and milder winters. Plan your journey appropriately, taking into account the ideal season to visit particular locales. For instance, to experience lush vegetation and waterfalls, travel to the southern Dhofar region during the Khareef (monsoon) season.

Respect Cultural Customs: Oman is a conservative nation with strong cultural customs. To guarantee a peaceful and respectful visit, observe regional traditions, dress modestly, and respect cultural norms.

Oman has superb luxury resorts and stunning beaches, so make sure to relax. Include some downtime and recharging in your schedule so that you may unwind and refresh.

You may immerse yourself in Oman's distinct charm, take in its natural beauty, and make lifelong memories by thoughtfully planning your travel itinerary.

2.4 Packing Essentials

It's crucial to pack sensibly while making travel plans to Oman, a nation renowned for its breathtaking scenery, ancient history, and rich culture, in order to ensure a comfortable and enjoyable stay. Here are some items you should carry for your trip to Oman, which offers a variety of desert experiences, seaside delights, and hilly terrains:

Lightweight, breathable clothing is recommended because Oman has a scorching, desert climate, particularly in the summer. To stay cool in the heat, bring lightweight, loose-fitting clothes that breathes well. You can avoid the sun's rays and probable mosquito bites in the evenings by wearing long sleeve shirts and slacks made of breathable materials.

Sun protection: Oman's sun can be very strong. Remember to bring lots of high SPF sunscreen, sunglasses with UV protection, and a wide-brimmed hat to protect yourself from the harsh sun's rays.

Swimwear and beach equipment: Oman's coastline is home to many stunning beaches. To enjoy the pristine seas and abundant marine life, remember to carry your swimsuit, beach towels, and snorkeling equipment.

Bring sturdy shoes that are comfy and ideal for walking and hiking. For exploring the rocky landscape and wadis (river valleys), sturdy sandals or closed-toe shoes with high traction are recommended.

Basic first aid supplies including sticky bandages, antiseptic wipes, painkillers, and any prescription prescriptions you might want should be packed. While there are pharmacies in major cities, you might not be able to easily access them in rural areas.

Electronics and Power Adapters: To capture the stunning Omani scenery, don't forget your camera or smartphone. To keep your electronics charged, don't forget to pack a power adaptor (Type C or G) compatible with the local outlets.

Carrying a reusable water bottle will help you stay hydrated when traveling. To guarantee you have access to clean drinking water, particularly on hikes, think about investing in a bottle with a built-in filter.

Cash and Credit Cards: Although credit cards are accepted in big cities, it is advised to have cash on hand for transactions in remote areas and small businesses. The Omani Rial (OMR) serves as the local currency.

Omani Attire: It's polite to wear a light scarf or shawl to cover your shoulders and arms if you intend to visit mosques or other conservative locations. If they desire a more comprehensive cultural experience, men might wish to think about traditional Omani dishdashas.

Pack your necessary personal hygiene items, such as hand sanitizer, wet wipes, and tissues, in case soap and water aren't easily available.

A convenient daypack or backpack will be useful for day trips, hiking, and excursions to historical sites.

Travel Paperwork and Copies: Ensure that you have all necessary travel papers, such as your passport, any required visas, travel insurance, and printed bookings. In case of loss or theft, it's also a good idea to retain digital duplicates of important documents.

You'll be well-equipped to enjoy Oman's beauty and adventures if you carry these necessities. While exploring this fascinating nation, keep in mind to respect regional traditions and customs.

2.5 Currency And Money Matter

Oman, a unique nation on the Arabian Peninsula's southeast coast, has a storied past and a booming economy today. The currency, which is at the center of the country's financial system and has a major impact on how the country handles its money, is central to this.

The Omani Rial, sometimes known as OMR or the symbol, is the official unit of exchange in Oman. The remainder is split up into 1000 baisa. The Omani Rial has a reputation for being one of the most valuable currencies in the world, which is a result of the nation's stable economy and responsible fiscal policies.
The Central Bank of Oman is in charge of issuing and governing the country's banknotes and coins. Banknotes

are available in a variety of denominations, including 1, 5, 10, 20, and 50 rials, and each one is printed with a portrait of the current Sultan along with images of well-known sites and traditional motifs. There are coins in the values of 5, 10, 25, 50, and 100 baisa that feature images from Oman's rich cultural past.

The Central Bank of Oman carefully crafts monetary policies to preserve price stability and long-term economic growth. The central bank efficiently manages inflation and exchange rates by regulating the money supply, interest rates, and foreign currency reserves. In order to promote a secure financial environment, it is crucial to regulate the nation's banking and financial institutions.

Economic Diversification: Oman's economy has historically been dependent on oil exports, but the government has recently placed a strong emphasis on broadening the country's economic basis. The goal of this diversification policy is to lessen the nation's reliance on oil revenue while fostering expansion in industries including tourism, manufacturing, logistics, and finance. A stable and sustainable economy has been made possible despite variations in the price of oil around the world thanks to this strategy.

Currency exchange and banking services: Oman has a thriving banking industry with a wide array of local and foreign banks. Travelers on vacation and on business can easily exchange their money for local currency thanks to the availability of facilities at airports, banks, exchange bureaus, and major commercial hubs.

2.6 Accommodation Options In Oman

Oman welcomes visitors with a variety of lodging options that fit a range of budgets and interests thanks to its fascinating scenery and lively culture. Here is a thorough directory of lodging options in Oman, along with rough price ranges, whether you're looking for luxury resorts, cultural excursions, or inexpensive stays:

Luxurious Resorts and Accommodations: Oman is home to a number of opulent beach resorts and accommodations, particularly in Muscat and adjacent coastal areas. These luxurious accommodations provide top-notch amenities, exclusive beaches, infinity pools, spa services, and exquisite dining options. Depending on the location, the time of year, and the level of extravagance, the cost of a luxury hotel room can range from $200 to $800 per night.

Boutique Hotels: These establishments are a great option for tourists looking for a more personal and culturally immersive stay. These lovely homes are located in old districts and frequently feature Omani architecture and design. Boutique hotels often cost between $100 and $250 per night.

Affordable and Mid-Range Hotels: Oman also offers a selection of affordable and mid-range hotels, notably in major cities and well-known tourist destinations. These motels provide cozy accommodations and necessary amenities at reasonable rates. Budget-conscious guests will find budget and midrange hotels to their liking because of their prices, which range from $50 to $150 a night.

Traditional Omani Guesthouses: To experience the real Omani way of life, think of staying in one of the "Al Wadi" traditional guesthouses. These family-run guesthouses provide an understanding of Omani culture, traditions, and cuisine. Al Wadi lodging costs typically range from $50 to $150 per night, depending on the location and amenities offered.

Eco-Lodges and Desert Camps: Eco-lodges and desert camps focus on sustainable practices and cater to tourists who love the outdoors. These lodgings provide breath-taking views and eco-aware experiences because they are tucked away in ecologically delicate places. Depending on location and level of quality, eco-lodges and desert camps can cost anywhere from $100 to $300 per night.

Glamping Locations: Glamping, or glam camping, is becoming more and more popular in Oman. These campgrounds offer a comfortable camping experience with cozy tents, decent beds, and contemporary conveniences. Glamping locations typically cost between $150 and $400 per night and provide a distinctive fusion of luxury and nature.

Airbnb and Vacation Rentals: As the sharing economy has grown, there are now more vacation rental alternatives available in Oman thanks to websites like Airbnb. For short-term stays, tourists can choose flats, villas, and houses that provide a more comfortable and adaptable experience. Depending on the location, size, and amenities, vacation rental prices can range from $50 to over $300 per night.

Hostels: Hostels are a reasonable choice for travellers on a tight budget and single travelers. The main tourist destinations in Oman now include hostels that offer inexpensive shared dormitory-style lodging. Hostels can be found for $20 to $50 per night, making them an affordable option for travelers on a limited budget.

CHAPTER THREE

Getting To Know Oman

3.1 Geography And Regions

Oman, also referred to as the Sultanate of Oman, is a fascinating and diversified nation that is situated in the southeast of the Arabian Peninsula. Its geographical features include fertile valleys, rocky mountains, pristine coasts, and desert landscapes. Oman, which has a total size of around 309,500 square kilometers, borders Yemen to the southwest, Saudi Arabia to the west, and the United Arab Emirates to the northwest. Oman is bordered by the Arabian Sea to the east and the strategically important Strait of Hormuz to the north.

The Al Hajar mountain range, which spans from the Musandam Peninsula in the north to the eastern shoreline, is the country's most notable geographical feature. These mountains rise steeply, in some places rising over 3,000 meters. With its fjord-like inlets and high cliffs, Musandam's northern section, which is isolated from the rest of Oman, has earned the moniker "Norway of the Middle East."

The bulk of Oman's people live in the coastal plains and valleys, where productive soils support date palm farming as well as other agricultural products including wheat and vegetables. The nation's political, economic, and cultural centers are located in Muscat, the capital city, which is found on the country's northern shore.

As you travel south down the coast, you'll pass by gorgeous fishing communities and large expanses of sand beaches that are bordered by the Arabian Sea. Oman is a well-liked vacation spot for divers thanks to the abundance of marine life in the waters nearby.

The huge Rub' al Khali, often known as the Empty Quarter, the world's biggest continuous sand desert, dominates the central and southern regions of Oman. The parched plains and undulating dunes of this difficult and dismal landscape stand in stark contrast to the northern green valleys.

The climate in Oman varies by region. While highland locations have a more temperate environment with cooler temperatures and infrequent rainfall, coastal areas enjoy a hot and humid climate. Deserts and other inland regions experience hot summers and mild winters.

To sum up, Oman's varied terrain offers an incredible variety of sceneries, from imposing mountains to immaculate coastlines and vast deserts. Travelers interested in discovering the treasures of the Arabian Peninsula will find the nation to be an intriguing destination due to its distinctive combination of natural beauty and cultural legacy.

3.2 Oman's Rich History And Culture

Oman is one of the oldest civilizations in the Arabian Peninsula, with a history and culture that span thousands of years. Because of the nation's advantageous location near historic trade routes and the Indian Ocean, cultural contact has been enabled and has shaped its growth.

Oman has a long history of serving as a crossroads for maritime trade between the East and West. Its sailors were expert navigators who built commercial ties with China, India, Persia, East Africa, and other far-off nations. The recognizable dhow boats of Oman, which are still used for fishing and cargo transportation today, are a reflection of this nautical legacy.

The Sultanate of Oman's rule in the 18th and 19th centuries was one of the most important eras in Oman's history. Oman developed into a maritime empire with lands extending along the east coast of Africa, including

Zanzibar and portions of Kenya, under the rule of the Al Said dynasty. Muscat, the nation's capital, was a thriving trading port with a strong naval presence that guaranteed Omani dominance in the trade of the Indian Ocean.

Islam has a strong hold on Oman's cultural heritage and has a major influence on how people live their everyday lives and observe rituals. Ibadi Islam is a distinctive branch of Islam that is practiced by the vast majority of people in Oman. Five times a day, the call to prayer is heard throughout Omani cities and towns, and mosques and religious schools (madrasas) are essential components of Omani communities.

Omanis are extremely proud of their traditions and rituals. Particularly in rural areas, traditional clothing, such as the dishdasha for men and the abaya for women, is frequently worn. East African, Indian, and Persian influences can be found in Omani cuisine, which reflects the nation's long history of trading. Shuwa (marinated beef cooked underground), mashuai (spit-roasted fish), and dates are popular foods that have special cultural and religious significance.

Beautifully preserved forts, castles, and watchtowers that serve as reminders of Oman's past defensive tactics make up the country's architectural legacy, which is highly remarkable. Among the most well-known examples are the forts of Nizwa, Bahla, and Jabrin.

The Razha, a vivacious sword dance, and the Liwa, a song-and-dance routine backed by drums and flutes, are examples of traditional performances that highlight the importance of music and dance to Omani culture. The value of poetry and narrative is great, and storytelling is a skill that has been passed down through the years.

The revival and preservation of Oman's cultural heritage have accelerated recently. To honor and promote the nation's legacy, organizations like the National Museum and the Royal Opera House Muscat have been formed. A part of Oman's intangible cultural legacy is the revival and appreciation of traditional crafts like weaving, ceramics, and silverwork.

Conclusion: Oman's strategic geographic location, maritime heritage, and rich history and culture are intricately entwined. The nation's dedication to upholding its traditions while embracing modernity makes it an alluring tourism destination and an illustrative case of Middle Eastern cultural continuity.

3.3 Traditional Omani Cuisine And Delicacies

The long history of trade and cultural interchange in Omani influences the delicious flavor fusion that is traditional cuisine. The numerous cultural influences from India, Persia, East Africa, and the Arabian Peninsula are reflected in the cuisine. The use of flavorful spices, tender meats, and a vast variety of ingredients from both the sea and the land make Omani cuisine famous.

"Shuwa" is one of the most well-known and adored Omani delicacies. It is customary to create this dish for festivities and important events. A whole lamb or goat is marinated in a mixture of spices, such as cinnamon, cardamom, and cloves, and then wrapped in banana or palm leaves for shouwa. The meat is then cooked underground over a long period of time, producing delicious, soft meat that easily slips off the bone. Shuwa is a time-consuming dish that is frequently prepared in big quantities to be shared with friends and family.

Omani cuisine emphasizes seafood heavily because of the country's wide coastline. A whole roasted fish, generally kingfish or shark, is served on top of seasoned rice in the traditional Omani meal known as "Mashuai". The fish is cooked until it is perfectly moist and tasty after being marinated with a specific mixture of spices, which includes dried limes and saffron. Fried onions are frequently used as a garnish, and a side of hot tomato sauce is frequently included.

Traditional Omani bread known as "rukhal" is created from unleavened dough that is rolled thin and heated on a hotplate. It is frequently eaten with a variety of side dishes, including cheese, honey, and ghee (clarified butter). In Oman, rakhal is a common dish that can be eaten as a snack or as a full meal.

Dates are given as a token of charity and hospitality in Oman, where they have a great cultural significance. Dates are often consumed as a sweet treat or added to cakes and pastries. There are many different varieties of dates farmed throughout the nation. A common traditional dessert called "halwa" is created with sugar, rosewater, saffron, ghee, and a variety of nuts and spices. The outcome is a rich, fragrant pastry that is frequently paired with coffee or tea.

Similar to biryani, "maqbous" or "makbous" is another traditional Omani dish. The dish is created with tender meat, frequently chicken or lamb, cooked with a mixture of veggies, almonds, and raisins. The rice is flavored. The meal is a mainstay at gatherings with family and special occasions since it is brimming with spices.

CHAPTER FOUR

Practical Information

4.1 Getting To Oman

Oman, an intriguing location with a rich history, stunning scenery, and welcoming locals, is located on the Arabian Peninsula's southeast coast. There are a number of easy ways for travelers to reach Oman before beginning their adventure to this jewel of the Arabian Peninsula.

Air Travel: Flying is the quickest and most popular method of getting to Oman. The primary entry point into the nation is the Sultan Qaboos International Airport, which is situated in Muscat, the capital. Major international airlines fly into this contemporary airport, making it reachable from many different corners of the globe. Regular flights to Oman are available from practically every region of the world, including Europe, Asia, Africa, and beyond.

Oman and Saudi Arabia, Yemen, and the United Arab Emirates (UAE) all share a land border. These land border crossings allow visitors from nearby nations or those taking a road trip to enter Oman. Before beginning this overland adventure, make sure you have all the required visas and documentation. It's also important to review the most recent border policies and safety recommendations.

Travel by sea is possible thanks to Oman's extensive coastline along the Arabian Sea. Cruise ships and commercial vessels can dock at the major ports of Salalah, Muscat, and Sohar. A growing number of people are taking cruises to Oman to see the country's rich nautical heritage and stunning coastline.

Check the requirements for your nationality before traveling to Oman in order to obtain a visa. Many nations offer the option of obtaining a visa upon arrival or applying for an electronic visa in advance, simplifying the admission procedure. Oman has made tremendous efforts to simplify its visa requirements in order to welcome visitors and promote travel to the nation.

Internal Transportation: Once in Oman, there are several ways to go around and see the varied landscapes of the nation. Renting a car gives you the freedom to travel to far-flung places, picturesque wadis, and quaint villages. As an alternative, large cities are connected by well-kept roadways and public transportation, which makes getting around less expensive.

Etiquette and Safety: Oman is renowned for its gracious hospitality and safety. It's important for visitors to respect regional traditions and customs. When going to mosques and other religious locations, especially, dress modestly. Although Omanis are generally kind and nice, it is polite to ask permission before taking pictures of citizens, especially women.

In summary, traveling to Oman is a smooth and enjoyable experience. Oman offers a fantastic voyage that will fascinate visitors and make them want to come back for more adventures in this Arabian gem because of its beautiful scenery, cultural treasures, and welcoming residents.

4.2 Transportation Options In Oman

Oman offers a wide range of transportation choices to discover its natural beauty. The country has a variety of landscapes, including mountains, deserts, and unspoiled coastlines. Oman offers simple and dependable transportation options, whether you're exploring the historic forts, Muscat, the country's bustling capital, or secret wadis.

Renting a car is one of the most common and versatile choices for tourists in Oman. At airports and in city centers, reputable foreign vehicle rental agencies are present. Driving in Oman is quite simple thanks to well-maintained roads and adequate signs. Just make sure you have an international driver's license and abide by the regulations of the road.

Taxis: In Oman's cities and towns, taxis are easily accessible. You may readily locate them in Muscat at hotels, shopping centers, and popular destinations. Taxis are a great option for quick trips inside of cities. To prevent any problems with fare bargaining, it is advised to only take meter-equipped, government-regulated taxis.

Public Buses: The Oman primary Transport Company (ONTC), the country's primary transportation provider, runs a network of buses that connects the country's principal cities and towns. The air-conditioned buses provide an economical means of transportation. Plan your trip appropriately, as they might not be as frequent or quick as other options.

Intercity Buses: In addition to the government-run transportation agency, private bus companies connect different parts of Oman. These buses are cozy and offer a great method to travel outside of the major cities in the nation.

Shared taxis, also referred to as "Baiza" or "Service Taxis," are frequently employed by locals and travelers on a tight budget. They run on set routes between cities and towns, and the fare is split among the passengers. Although they can be a little crowded, shared cabs are a real way to see how locals live.

Domestic Flights: Oman's domestic flights are an easy alternative if you wish to go over big distances swiftly. Domestic flights from Muscat to important cities including Salalah, Sohar, and Duqm are offered by Oman Air and SalamAir. These brief flights provide breathtaking aerial views of Oman's varied landscapes.

Ferries: Oman, which has a long coastline, offers ferry services that link the country's capital, Muscat, to a number of coastal settlements and islands. Ferries are a fun way to go to some of Oman's picturesque beaches and fishing communities.

4.3 Staying Connected: Internet And Communication

Keeping in touch with loved ones, colleagues, and coworkers when on the road is crucial in the present digital era, and Oman offers good options for internet connection and communication. Oman provides dependable and effective connectivity alternatives for both inhabitants and visitors as a technologically evolved nation.

Widespread internet access is available across Oman, especially in urban areas and popular tourist locations. Hotels, cafes, and restaurants all have high-speed internet access, making it simple for visitors to access the internet and maintain connections. The nation's dedication to improving its digital infrastructure has given visitors a flawless internet experience.

SIM Cards & Mobile Data: Purchasing a local SIM card is a practical choice for tourists who want ongoing connectivity. Pre-paid SIM cards with varying data packages are available from telecommunications companies like Omantel and Ooredoo to meet a range of needs. Airports, convenience stores, and official outlets are all convenient places to get these SIM cards.

Wi-Fi Hotspots: In Oman, there are a lot of public locations with free Wi-Fi hotspots, including airports, shopping centers, and tourist destinations. Wi-Fi access is frequently available in inns, coffee shops, and dining establishments. Visitors can use these hotspots to stay connected without using their mobile data while exploring the cities.

Internet Cafes: In most cities and towns, there are internet cafes for tourists who don't have access to their own equipment or who require a prolonged internet session. These coffee shops feature high-speed internet connection in addition to frequently having printing and scanning capabilities.

VoIP & Messaging Apps: Although Oman provides dependable traditional phone services, many locals and visitors utilize VoIP services like WhatsApp, Skype, and FaceTime for international calls and video chats. It's important to note that some VoIP services can be limited in Oman, so it's a good idea to check the most recent rules.

Postal Services: Oman's postal services are effective and dependable, enabling visitors to send notes, packages, or postcards to friends, family members, or business associates. Most cities and towns have post offices, and possibilities for international shipping are widely accessible.

Emergency Contact Information: Oman has a well-respected emergency response system. Police, ambulance, and fire services can all be reached by dialling 999, which is also the general emergency number.

4.4 Health And Safety Tips

Although Oman is a secure and friendly destination for tourists, it's important to be aware of a few health and safety precautions to guarantee a hassle-free and pleasurable trip.

Make sure you have adequate travel insurance that covers medical emergencies, trip cancellations, and other unforeseen events before you depart for Oman. This will give you assurance during your journey.

Immunizations: To make sure you are up to date on routine immunizations, check with your doctor or a travel clinic. Additional immunizations including those for hepatitis A, typhoid, and tetanus may be advised based on your travel plans and medical background.

Hydration is important because Oman's climate is dry and hot, especially in the summer. Stay hydrated by consuming lots of water, and limit your time in the sun, particularly between the hours of 10 AM and 4 PM.

Sun Protection: Wear sunglasses, a wide-brimmed hat, and sunscreen with a high SPF to shield yourself from the harsh sun's rays. Wearing clothing that is light and loose-fitting can also keep you comfy.

Oman is a conservative nation with long-standing customs, so respect them. When visiting mosques and other religious buildings, show respect for local traditions by dressing modestly.

Driving in Oman? Be careful on the roads if you intend to drive. Be cautious when driving, always buckle up, and be aware of potential dangers, especially in remote areas.

Water Safety: Oman's wadis (natural pools) and shoreline are ideal for activities involving the water. However, when swimming or taking part in water activities, use caution and follow all safety precautions.

Water and Food: The local cuisine in Oman is delicious. Consider eating well-cooked and freshly prepared meals when touring eateries and street cuisine. Avoid ingesting ice from unidentified sources or tap water; instead, drink bottled water.

Keep abreast on the most recent COVID-19 guidelines and restrictions released by the Omani government while the epidemic is still in effect. Follow mask-wearing regulations and uphold your social distance in public.

Travelers may fully immerse themselves in Oman's rich culture, breathtaking landscapes, and warm hospitality while ensuring a safe and pleasant trip by keeping in mind these health and safety recommendations.

4.5 Language And Useful Phrases

Although English is commonly spoken, learning a few basic Arabic words can improve your trip experience and help you better understand the local way of life. Arabic is the official language of Oman. Arabic greetings and expressions can enhance relationships because Omanis are renowned for their friendly hospitality. Here are some helpful Arabic expressions to get about Oman:

Greetings:

Hello: مرحباً (Marhaba)

Good morning: صباح الخير (Sabah al-khayr)

Good afternoon: مساء الخير (Masa' al-khayr)
Good evening: مساء النور (Masa' al-noor)

How are you?: كيف حالك؟ (Kayfa halak?)

I'm fine, thank you: أنا بخير، شكراً (Ana bikhair, shukran)

Polite Expressions:

Please: من فضلك (Min fadlik)

Thank you: شكراً (Shukran)

You're welcome: عفواً (Afwan)

Excuse me: عذراً (Athirann)

Basic Conversations:

What is your name?: ما اسمك؟ (Ma ismuka?)

My name is...: اسمي... (Ismi...)

Where is...?: أين...؟ (Ayna...?)

How much is this?: بكم هذا؟ (Bikam hatha?)

Yes: نعم (Na'am)
No: لا (La)

Directions:

Go straight: اذهب مباشرةً (Ithhab mubashiran)

Turn left: انعطف يساراً (In'taf yasara)
Turn right: انعطف يميناً (In'taf yameenan)

Stop here: توقف هنا (Tawaqqaf huna)

Shopping:

How much does this cost?: كم يكلف هذا؟ (Kam yukallif hatha?)

Can you give me a discount?: هل يمكنك أن تعطيني خصم؟ (Hal yumkinuka an ta'teeni khasm?)

I want this: أريد هذا (Aureedu hatha)

I don't want this: لا أريد هذا (La aureedu hatha)

Learning a few Arabic phrases will not only enhance your travel experience in Oman but also show respect to the local culture and people. Omanis will appreciate your efforts, and these simple phrases can lead to memorable and meaningful interactions during your time in this enchanting Arabian destination.

4.6 Tips For Saving Money

For people of Oman, saving money is equally important for future ambitions and financial security. There are many methods to save money in this Middle Eastern nation with its developing economy and varied culture. Here are some thorough suggestions to help you cut costs in Oman:

Budgeting is Crucial: Make a monthly budget that details your revenue and outgoing costs. Don't forget to budget for things like housing, utilities, food, and transportation. To stop going overboard, stick to your spending plan.

Utilize Discounts: Keep an eye out for sales, discounts, and other promotional deals. The shopping scene in Oman is thriving, and you can save a lot of money by purchasing goods during sales or by using loyalty cards in stores and supermarkets.

Use Public Transportation: Oman has a sophisticated and economical public transportation system. To save money on gasoline and maintenance, use buses or shared taxis over own vehicles.

Energy Conservation: Oman endures hot weather all year round. To lower electricity costs, use energy-efficient appliances, turn off lights and electronics when not in use, and think about buying a programmable thermostat.

Prepare Meals at Home: Eating out can be costly, so try to make meals at home. You can save time and money by purchasing your goods in bulk and preparing your meals in advance.

Keep Hydrated Wisely: Oman's weather can be extremely hot and expensive water usage. Instead of frequently purchasing bottled water, choose reusable water bottles and fill them at water dispensers.

Discover Free Activities: Oman's diverse cultural legacy and stunning natural surroundings provide a variety of free activities. Without breaking the bank, take advantage of the beaches, go hiking, to museums, and check out neighborhood events.

Consider Second-Hand Purchases: If you're looking for furniture, gadgets, or apparel, consider buying used items. A broad variety of used items in good condition are available at a fraction of the price of new ones on websites and in nearby stores.

Avoid Impulsive Buying: Consider your options before making any unnecessary purchases. Avoid making impulsive purchases and consider whether you actually require the item or whether it is merely a passing desire.

Spend less on Healthcare: To offset potentially significant medical bills, purchase health insurance. Utilize free healthcare resources and preventative steps to lower your risk of needing expensive treatments.

Consolidate Debt: If you have several loans or credit card debts, you might want to think about combining them into one loan with a reduced interest rate so that your payments are easier to manage and you can save money on interest fees.

You may reach your long-term goals and establish a solid financial foundation by implementing these money-saving strategies into your daily life while still taking advantage of Oman's natural beauty and experiences.

CHAPTER FIVE

Muscat - The Capital Of Contrasts

5.1 Exploring Muscat's Top Attractions

Muscat is a wonderful city that skillfully combines historic charm with contemporary refinement. It is located along the beautiful coastline of Oman. This vibrant capital's centuries-old history is reflected in its stunning architecture, lively souks, and historical sites. A thrilling adventure that reveals the essence of Oman's rich tradition and natural beauty is discovering the top attractions in Muscat.

The Sultan Qaboos Grand Mosque is among the city's most recognizable monuments. This majestic building, with its lavish marble exterior, soaring minarets, and elaborate Islamic decorations, stands as a tribute to Oman's commitment to its faith and culture. Inside, there are magnificent chandeliers, including one of the largest in the world, as well as a remarkable prayer hall with elaborate carpeting and beautiful calligraphy.

Visit the Royal Opera House Muscat for a sample of the history and culture of the city. This architectural wonder offers a range of acts, from world-class operas to traditional dance shows, and displays a combination of contemporary and traditional Omani design. Another treasure that allows tourists to meander through exquisitely groomed gardens, see native plant species, and take a break from the bustle of the city is the calm Royal Botanical Garden.

The Mutrah Corniche is one of the most recognizable of Muscat's coastal features and part of the city's attractiveness. This vibrant promenade features a wonderful blend of old and modern architecture and runs beside the emerald waters of the Gulf of Oman. Explore the bustling Mutrah Souq to find a treasure trove of unique spices, handicrafts, and jewelry while taking a leisurely stroll and indulging in delectable Omani cuisine at waterfront eateries.

The Al Jalali and Al Mirani forts are intriguing reminders of the city's military heritage for history buffs. These magnificent buildings overlook the port and provide breath-taking views of the surrounding countryside and ocean. The National Museum, which has a large collection of relics, exhibitions, and interactive displays highlighting the country's cultural development, allows visitors to explore Oman's nautical heritage.

Last but not least, visiting Muscat wouldn't be complete without taking in the breathtaking shoreline. For soaking up the sun, swimming in the clean waters, or engaging in water activities like snorkeling and diving, head to the Bander Al Jissah and Qurum beaches.

5.2 Souks, Bazaars, And Shopping

Through its ancient souks and bazaars, Oman, a nation renowned for its rich history and colorful culture, provides a wonderful shopping experience. These markets serve as both shopping venues and a glimpse into Omani artistry and heritage. Inherent to Omani culture are souks and bazaars, where both locals and visitors go to take in the vibrant atmosphere and find one-of-a-kind treasures.

The Mutrah Souk in Muscat is one of Oman's most well-known souks. This souk is a sensory delight with its winding lanes, active shops, and alluring scents. A wide variety of traditional Omani goods are available for purchase, including handcrafted ceramics, frankincense, embroidered linens, and finely created silver jewelry. Friendly haggling is a common activity during shopping at the Mutrah Souk, making it a great spot to hone your bargaining skills.

The Nizwa Souq, which is situated in the historic city of Nizwa, is yet another important market. This souk is well-known for its Friday cattle market, when villagers congregate to exchange livestock and offer an insight into the history of the nation's agriculture. Visitors can browse stalls selling spices, traditional Omani daggers (khanjars), antiques, and vibrant souvenirs in addition to the cattle market.

The bazaars in Oman provide a unique opportunity for cultural immersion beyond simple shopping. Local craftsmen frequently display their talents, such as weaving traditional baskets or creating beautiful silver jewelry. A deeper understanding of Omani workmanship and the commitment behind each product results from this engagement with talented craftsmen.

These souks frequently have lively atmospheres that are alive with local music and conversation. Visitors may be asked to partake in Omani hospitality while visiting the busy marketplaces, with sellers providing dates, Omani coffee, and hydrating rosewater drinks.

Shopping at the souks and bazaars of Oman is a memorable experience, but it's important to respect regional traditions and customs. When in more conventional settings, dress modestly. Always get permission before snapping photos, especially of people.

Consequently, Oman's souks, bazaars, and shopping offer a remarkable fusion of conventional trade, cultural immersion, and a trip into the nation's rich legacy. The souks and bazaars of Oman are guaranteed to leave you with lasting memories of this fascinating country, whether you're looking for one-of-a-kind souvenirs, genuine Omani crafts, or simply want to soak up the vibrant atmosphere.

5.3 Where To Stay: Accommodation Options

The capital of Oman, Muscat, provides a wide variety of lodging choices to fit any traveler's needs and price range. Muscat offers accommodations for every budget, from opulent beachside resorts to charming boutique hotels and affordable guesthouses.

Luxury Resorts: Muscat is home to a number of top-tier resorts, many of which are found along the breathtaking coastline. These hotels include lavish amenities, exclusive beaches, infinity pools, spa services, and an abundance of eating choices. The Chedi Muscat, Al Bustan Palace, and Shangri-La Barr Al Jissah Resort & Spa are a few well-known examples of luxury resorts.

Travelers looking for a more personalized and distinctive experience might consider Muscat's boutique hotels. These more intimate businesses frequently use traditional Omani architecture and provide individualized services. The View, Hud Hud Boutique Hotels, and Al Maha International Hotel are three exquisite boutique hotels to take into account.

Hotels in the City Center: The city center of Muscat offers quick access to the city's top sights, malls, and eateries. In this region, there are several hotels that cater to both business and leisure guests and provide cutting-edge conveniences. The Radisson Blu Hotel, Grand Millennium Muscat, and Centara Hotels & Resorts Muscat are a few choices.

Beachfront Properties: Beautiful beachfront hotels can be found all along Muscat's coastline, giving visitors the chance to awaken to mesmerizing views of the Arabian Sea. These resorts frequently provide a variety of water sports and seaside leisure. Crowne Plaza Muscat, Sheraton Oman Hotel, and Sheraton Oman Beach Resort are a few well-known seaside hotels.

Budget travelers or those looking for a more comfortable setting might consider Muscat's guesthouses or serviced flats. These lodgings offer a cozy stay with simple facilities, making them perfect for families or frequent travelers.

Accommodations in a traditional Omani guesthouse or a desert tent would make for a more authentic experience. These lodgings give visitors the chance to become fully immersed in local culture and the Omani way of life.

Regardless of your decision, it's imperative to reserve lodging in advance, especially during busy travel times. The hospitality sector in Muscat is renowned for its kind and inviting character, which makes sure that every visitor has a wonderful time while visiting this stunning city. Whatever level of elegance, authenticity, or affordability you desire, Muscat offers a variety of lodging choices to make your trip to Oman really unforgettable.

5.4 Culinary Delights In Muscat

Oman's capital city, Muscat, is known for its delectable fusion of traditional Omani cuisine, foreign cuisines, and cutting-edge eating experiences. The city's diversified culinary culture offers something for every palate, making it a paradise for foodies.

Omani Food: Authentic Omani cuisine is one of the attractions of eating in Muscat. Infused with a complex mixture of spices and herbs, local recipes frequently incorporate rice, fish, and meat. Shuwa, a slow-cooked marinated lamb or goat dish that is usually prepared underground and yields soft, flavorful meat, is a must-try Omani specialty. Other popular Omani dishes include Harees (a meal consisting of wheat and meat), Mashuai (grilled fish eaten with rice), and Majboos (spiced rice with meat or fish).

Seafood: Muscat has an abundance of fresh seafood because it is a coastal city. You may savor exquisite Omani lobster, prawns, crab, and a variety of fish that has been served either in a typical Omani style or in a foreign style. The vivid and genuine experience can be found at the fish markets close to Mutrah Corniche.

Cuisine from throughout the world is available in a variety of restaurants in Muscat, which also caters to international preferences. You can get a variety of flavors to sate your appetites, from Italian, French, and American to Thai, Lebanese, and Indian.

Omani Sweets: Enjoying Omani Sweets is a delicious delicacy that shouldn't be missed. Local favorites include Omani dates, which are renowned as some of the best in the world, and Halwa, a sweet confection made with rosewater, saffron, and nuts.

Street Food: Investigate the city's street food culture for a real culinary experience. Samosas, Omani Bread (Rghag), and Shawarma are just a few of the snacks and sweets that can be found on the streets of Muscat from food stalls and merchants.

Fine Dining: There are a number of expensive restaurants in Muscat that provide fine dining experiences with faultless service and imaginative, gourmet fare. Numerous of these eateries have breathtaking views of the city or the ocean, which improves the whole dining experience.

Omani Coffee: In Omani culture, coffee has a unique place. Don't pass up the chance to sample Omani coffee, a traditional brew that is served with dates and cardamom.

CHAPTER SIX

The Natural Wonders Of Oman

6.1 Desert Adventures In Wahiba Sands

The captivating Wahiba Sands, a vast desert that runs for more than 125 miles and offers adventurous travelers an exceptional experience in the Arabian Peninsula, are tucked away in the heart of Oman. A thrilling voyage into a world of massive dunes, illustrious customs, and stunning scenery is promised by Oman Desert Adventures at Wahiba Sands.

Adventurers are greeted by a mesmerizing vision of undulating sands as the sun rises over the golden dunes, with each ripple narrating the story of the ancient winds that sculpted this breathtaking landscape. Visitors have the option to partake in a variety of activities, starting with dune bashing, to completely immerse themselves in the desert experience. Powerful 4x4 vehicles are driven through the sand dunes by skilled drivers, providing thrill-seekers with an exhilarating rollercoaster ride. The exhilarating experience of ascending the high dunes and dashing down their slopes is unmatched.

Camels offer a serene and genuine experience for anyone looking for a more traditional interaction. Assisted by local Bedouin guides, tourists ride slowly camels across the vast desert while the soft sway of the animal's gait calms their souls.

A tranquil serenity permeates the desert as the day transitions into the evening. It's the ideal moment to witness a spectacular sunset. A moment of complete peace and unadulterated beauty, when the sun dips below the horizon and the sky turns shades of orange and pink, will live in one's memory forever.

The real wonder starts when night falls upon the Wahiba Sands. The night sky becomes a heavenly painting, sparkling with stars that are untarnished by city light pollution. Stargazing in the desert provides a unique opportunity to interact with the sky and exposes an astounding variety of constellations.

Visitors can choose to spend the night in authentic Bedouin-style desert camps to round off their desert journey. With warm traditional Arabian hospitality, delectable regional cuisine, and cultural acts like folk music and dance, these camps offer a relaxing and genuine experience. Travelers can learn about the Bedouins' time-honored customs and distinctive way of life by listening to their tales while gathered around a roaring campfire.

A voyage into the heart of the Arabian desert is truly offered by Oman Desert Adventures in Wahiba Sands. It is evidence of the mesmerizing natural beauty and the extensive cultural history of Oman, where tradition and modernity coexist together. Travelers are guaranteed to return home from a trip to this enchanted land with priceless memories and a newfound respect for nature's charms.

6.2 Jewel Of The Arabian Peninsula: Wadi Shab

The breathtaking natural beauty known as Wadi Shab is located in the remote Sharqiyah district of Oman, tucked hidden amid the region's rough terrain. This gorgeous location, which is frequently referred to as the "Jewel of the Arabian Peninsula," is a veritable paradise for nature lovers and adventure seekers alike.

Wadi Shab, which means "Gorge between Cliffs" in Arabic, is a valley or dry riverbed encircled by rugged mountains and dizzying cliffs. Wadi Shab is reached after a picturesque drive through the Omani countryside that passes through small towns and date palm plantations. The scenery changes as you go closer to the wadi into an alluring arrangement of emerald-green oases, crystal-clear lakes, and limestone rocks.

It is possible to go hiking and swimming in Wadi Shab, which is one of its main draws. The excursion begins with a leisurely walk through the wadi's stony trail, which is shaded by hanging ferns and palm palms. The journey gets harder as you travel deeper into the canyon because you have to scramble over boulders and wade across little pools of water. The journey itself is an adventure, and as you near the Wadi Shab gem, the excitement grows.

Visitors arrive at the main attraction after an energizing hike: a secret lake that sparkles like a sapphire among the golden canyon walls. A sequence of flowing waterfalls feed the natural pool, providing an exquisite and dreamlike environment. It's breathtaking to see the turquoise seas set against the stark backdrop of the jagged cliffs, which also serves as an alluring call to go swimming. Swimmers can plunge into the chilly water and through a short crack to expose a little cavern that adds to the attraction of the location.

Wadi Shab provides an extra reward for those with a greater sense of adventure. There is a secret cave that can be explored beyond the pool. Swimmers must take a deep breath before diving underwater to reach there. They must then swim through a small tunnel that leads to an underground cavern. The sole light in the cave is a tiny hole in the roof that shines a lovely glow on the water. Those who are willing to take the risk are rewarded with an incredible experience.

In addition to its stunning natural beauty, Wadi Shab provides a haven for nearby species and a vibrant ecosystem. Visitors with keen eyes may see several bird types, freshwater fish, and if they're lucky, the elusive Arabian leopard.

Wadi Shab is proof of Oman's unrivaled natural beauty and its status as an undiscovered jewel in the Arabian Peninsula. All who visit are enchanted by the harmonious combination of craggy cliffs, rich flora, and crystal-clear waterways that produces an unforgettable experience. Wadi Shab promises an extraordinary voyage that will leave an imprint on your soul, whether you're looking for adventure, tranquillity, or simply a connection with nature.

7.3 Coastal Charms: Salalah And Dhofar Region

The coastal city of Salalah and the adjacent Dhofar region are situated in southern Oman and resemble an undiscovered treasure. This captivating location stands out from the rest of the Arabian Peninsula thanks to its special combination of unmatched natural beauty, extensive history, and vibrant culture.

Salalah and Dhofar's lush vegetation and temperate climate, which strongly contrast with the dry desert vistas normally associated with Oman, are two of its most alluring features. The Khareef season, a monsoon season that lasts from June to September, is thought to be responsible for this phenomena. The area goes through a remarkable transition during this season, with the parched mountains and valleys being covered in a beautiful carpet of greenery. A natural refuge of tranquility and beauty, the surroundings come to life with flowing waterfalls, meandering streams, and blossoming flowers.

Al Mughsayl Beach in the Dhofar region is a must-see destination because of its blowholes. Water is forced through the holes when the waves smash against the limestone cliffs, resulting in stunning geysers that can soar up to 30 meters in height. Visitors come from all over the world to see this captivating natural phenomenon.

In addition, Salalah has a rich cultural heritage that is firmly based in its maritime past and extensive trading relations. The ancient city of Zafar, which dates to the eighth century, is displayed at the Al Baleed Archaeological Park, a UNESCO World Heritage site. Discover more about Oman's past as a significant hub of trade and civilisation by visiting the archaeological museum, huge mosque, and well-preserved remnants of the citadel.

The traditional Omani souqs (markets), where visitors may experience local culture and find one-of-a-kind handicrafts, spices, and frankincense, an ancient aromatic resin highly valued in ancient trade, are another fascinating feature of Salalah and Dhofar. Particularly crowded and full of pottery, colorful linens, and finely wrought silver jewelry is the Haffa Souq.

The Dhofar Mountains must be visited by anyone who loves the outdoors. These untamed mountains, which tower above the surroundings, offer stunning hiking paths that offer expansive views of the countryside and the Indian Ocean. You may come across traditional Omani villages while you explore the highlands, where you may enjoy the warm hospitality of the residents and discover more about their way of life.

The seaside attractions of Oman in Salalah and the Dhofar region provide a wealth of unique adventures. This region of the Arabian Peninsula offers a distinctive and varied trip for those looking to take the less-traveled path, from the lush greenery during the Khareef season to the historical gems and inviting communities.

6.4 Discovering Jebel Akhdar And Jebel Shams

The magnificent Jebel Akhdar and Jebel Shams mountains are where Oman's untamed beauty is at its most breathtaking. Travelers have a unique opportunity to discover the nation's varied landscapes, from lush terraced orchards to deep canyons that rival the world's largest canyons, thanks to these two prominent peaks.

The "Green Mountain," also known as Jebel Akhdar, is a mountain range in northeastern Oman that is a part of the Al Hajar mountain range. Its name is appropriately derived from the luxuriant plantations and terraced farms that adorn its slopes and are maintained by the brilliant Falaj irrigation system. The mountain is a great place to escape the sweltering Omani summers because of the cooler temperatures there. Hiking tours through the scenic villages, like Al Ayn and Wadi Bani Habib, where the ancient Omani way of life has been maintained for decades, are available to tourists. The beautiful Damask roses are grown at Jebel Akhdar's rose gardens, which are also where the renowned Omani rose water is made. The mountains are covered in pink and white blooms between March and April each year, giving the area an ethereal atmosphere.

On the other hand, Jebel Shams, also known as the "Mountain of the Sun," is one of Oman's highest points and the tallest peak in the Al Hajar range, rising more than 3,000 meters above sea level. With various trekking trails leading to the rim of the "Grand Canyon of Oman," known as Wadi Ghul, the rocky landscape of Jebel Shams provides fascinating prospects for adventurers. Even more impressive than the Grand Canyon in the United States, this magnificent canyon's towering walls and beautiful views will astound anyone who visits.

Jebel Shams also provides chances for rock climbing and abseiling down its sheer cliff faces for those wanting an adrenaline rush, making for an amazing journey for adventure seekers.

Both Jebel Akhdar and Jebel Shams provide unmatched astronomy chances in addition to their magnificent vistas. Away from city lights, the starry night skies offer a captivating view of the constellations, Milky Way, and other stars, luring visitors to consider the size of the universe.

The mountainous treasures of Oman entice adventurers and nature lovers to discover the incredible diversity of the Arabian Peninsula's landscapes, whether it is the serene allure of terraced orchards in Jebel Akhdar or the breathtaking majesty of the canyon in Jebel Shams. Traveling to Jebel Akhdar and Jebel Shams, where the enduring beauty of nature converges with the rich tapestry of Omani heritage and culture, promises to be a life-changing experience.

CHAPTER SEVEN

Historical Treasures And Cultural Gems

7.1 Nizwa - A Glimpse Into The Past

A fascinating look into the Sultanate of Oman's rich history and cultural heritage may be had by travelers in the city of Nizwa. Nizwa offers a singular fusion of the past and present since it is steeped in ancient traditions and surrounded by breathtaking scenery.

The Nizwa Fort, which showcases Oman's architectural brilliance, is the city's most recognizable monument. The fort, which was constructed in the 17th century, was crucial to the region's defense against invaders and served as a bastion for the ruling dynasty. Its imposing walls, strong towers, and elaborate wooden doors demonstrate the creativity of Omani artisans of that time. Visitors can explore its confusing passages and hidden chambers inside, as well as view exhibitions and displays that provide information about the city's fascinating history.

The lively Nizwa Souq, a dynamic market that has been operating for generations, is within a short distance from the fort. As visitors stroll through the quaint alleyways lined with vibrant kiosks selling fresh food, silverware, spices, and traditional Omani crafts, they are immediately taken back in time. The ambience of the souq is reminiscent of the past with the sounds of bargaining traders and the perfume of exotic spices.

The city of Nizwa's dedication to upholding regional traditions and rituals is among its most alluring features. The region's agricultural has been supported for decades by the city's famed traditional falaj irrigation system, a clever network of underground channels. Observing the falaj system's fine detail brings to light the continuing knowledge of earlier generations and their capacity to adapt to the difficult desert environment.

The historic Jabrin Castle, another exquisite example of 17th-century architecture, is another attraction in Nizwa. This magnificent building, which previously served as a hub for learning and intellectual pursuits, is home to delicately adorned ceilings, elaborate carvings, and stunning murals that provide insight into the artistic prowess of earlier Omani craftsmen.

In addition to its historical assets, Nizwa's surroundings provide an intriguing contrast. There are many options for trekking and exploring in the adjacent Jebel Akhdar Mountains, which juxtapose the dry desert plains with terraced farms and lush vegetation.

Nizwa is a living example of Oman's rich historical and cultural legacy, to sum up. The city provides visitors an incredible trip back in time and a great respect for the heritage of the past that still exists in the present with its well-preserved architectural marvels, bustling souq, ancient irrigation systems, and stunning scenery.

7.2 Bahla And Jabreen: Fortresses And Castles

The Bahla and Jabreen castles and fortifications in Oman are two remarkable historical locations that offer a fascinating look at the nation's impressive architectural prowess and rich cultural legacy. These UNESCO World Heritage Sites are among of the most significant and well-preserved fortifications in the Arabian Peninsula and are situated in the center of Oman, close to the city of Nizwa.

The Bahla Fort, sometimes called "Jabrin Castle," was built in the 13th century and serves as a reminder of Oman's historical military prowess and strategic importance. The fort's enormous mud-brick walls, which are almost 7 miles long and up to 50 feet tall, are a magnificent example of the creativity of Omani builders in the past. Bahla Fort, one of Oman's oldest and biggest forts, was formerly the seat of the Nabhani dynasty and was essential in securing the trade routes that passed through the area.

On the other side, Jabreen Castle is a magnificent example of medieval Islamic architecture. The castle, which was constructed in the 17th century, doubled as a place of learning and intellectual pursuits. Its spectacular interior displays the artistic and architectural prowess of that time period with its complex wood carvings, gorgeously painted ceilings, and fine stucco work. The majestic great hall and the tower, which provides sweeping views of the surroundings, are only two of the several chambers that guests can see inside the castle.

Bahla and Jabreen both have distinctive falaj systems that are reminiscent of traditional Omani water management practices. For ages, the region's ancient irrigation systems have played a crucial role in sustaining agriculture, demonstrating the creativity and knowledge of earlier generations.

The public can now visit the strongholds and castles at Bahla and Jabreen, which offer a magnificent tour through Oman's history and culture. Wandering through the beautifully preserved courtyards, towers, and halls allows visitors to experience the atmosphere of bygone ages. The experience is both instructive and fascinating thanks to the informational exhibits and guided tours that provide insights into the historical significance of these locations.

The strongholds and castles at Bahla and Jabreen, which serve as enduring representations of Oman's architectural heritage and cultural legacy, are two of the country's most impressive historical assets. In addition to awe-inspiring tourists with their grandeur and historical significance, these sites provide a greater understanding of Oman's past, its military strength, and its distinctive water management strategies that have supported life in this dry region for generations.

7.3 Rustaq's Hot Springs And Rich Heritage

The Sultanate of Oman's scenic village of Rustaq is well known for its hot springs and extensive cultural history. Rustaq, tucked away in the Hajar Mountains, provides tourists with a singular and restorative experience through its natural thermal waters and a strong link to the nation's past.

The Ain Al Kasafa hot springs, sometimes referred to as the Rustaq hot springs, are one of the primary attractions in Rustaq. Since these healing waters have been utilized for generations and are thought to provide treatment from a number of ailments, both locals and visitors looking to unwind and improve their wellness frequently visit them. Visitors can unwind and soak in the relaxing waters at the hot springs, which are encircled by beautiful vegetation.

Beyond its natural splendors, Rustaq is home to many well-preserved landmarks that reflect a rich historical past. The town is home to the majestic Rustaq Fort, a building from pre-Islamic times that was important to Oman's history. The fort was originally home to Oman's ruling class and protected the city from attackers with its towering walls and watchtowers. The fort still stands as a tribute to the area's architectural skill and provides sweeping vistas of the surroundings.

The Nakhal Fort, built on a rocky hill overlooking date plantations and the oasis, is another significant historical landmark in Rustaq. Pre-Islamic in origin and later renovated throughout the Islamic era, the Nakhal Fort is a fortification that has been magnificently restored. It offers tourists a look at Oman's rich cultural heritage and architectural traditions by showcasing beautiful woodwork, ornamental arches, and elaborate balconies.

The historic souqs in Rustaq, where tourists may immerse themselves in the lively atmosphere of local marketplaces, are also part of the city's cultural legacy. Particularly active for generations, the Al Hazm Souq offers a lovely selection of traditional Omani handicrafts, spices, textiles, and jewelry, offering a window into the town's commercial history.

Festivals and other customary occasions in the community provide an additional way to take in Rustaq's rich history. One of the many lively cultural events that highlights Oman's deeply ingrained customs and traditions is the yearly Eid Al Fitr celebrations. Another is the Al Ardha dance, a traditional sword dance.

7.4 Sur And The Seafaring Traditions

Due to its long history of seafaring, Sur, a coastal city in the Sultanate of Oman, is noteworthy in the history of the nation. Sur, a major maritime center renowned for its shipbuilding expertise and maritime commerce operations, is located on the eastern coast of Oman.

The city has a lengthy nautical history that dates back to the sixth century, when Sur served as a strategic port on the old maritime Silk Road. Sur's natural harbor attracted traders from all over the world as a gateway to India, Africa, and other continents, adding to the city's multicultural ambiance.

The classic Omani dhow is one of Sur's most recognizable representations of its maritime heritage. These unusual triangular-sailed wooden sailing vessels have been made in Sur for many centuries. The city's shipbuilding sector is known for its skill and workmanship, using age-old methods that have been handed down through families for millennia. At Sur's shipyards, visitors may observe the shipbuilding process and learn about the meticulous craftsmanship involved in building these seagoing warships.

The Sur marine Museum provides a thorough understanding of the city's marine customs and history. The museum's displays feature replicas of historic dhows, nautical equipment, and maritime trade relics and take visitors on a fascinating tour of Sur's seafaring past.

The yearly Al-Maktoum traditional sailing competition, when local fishermen compete in their dhows to show off their talents and honor the nautical legacy of their forefathers, is another example of Sur's continuous connection to the sea.

The city's stunning beaches and crystal-clear waters offer plenty of chances for tourists to engage in different water sports, such as fishing, sailing, and diving. Visitors can see Sur's lively fish market, where the day's catch is sold at auction, where fishing is still a key component of the local economy.

Ras Al Hadd and Ras Al Jinz, which are close by and renowned for being green turtle nesting grounds, share Sur's coastal attractiveness. These locations provide a rare opportunity to see these amazing creatures lay eggs and watch baby turtles develop.

In conclusion, Oman's history and cultural identity have been irrevocably shaped by Sur's maritime traditions. The city's nautical tradition continues to flourish, encouraging tourists to immerse themselves in the fascinating world of Oman's maritime past and present, from the renowned dhows and shipbuilding expertise to the busy fish market and immaculate turtle nesting places.

CHAPTER EIGHT

Outdoor Activities And Adventure

8.1 Diving and Snorkeling In Oman's Pristine Waters

Divers and snorkelers will find Oman's clear waters to be a mesmerizing paradise. This charming nation, which is located along the Arabian Peninsula's southeast coast, has a gorgeous coastline that stretches for more than 2,000 kilometers and is graced with undeveloped beaches, bright coral reefs, and a varied marine life. Oman is a veritable sanctuary for underwater explorers with its clean waters, teeming marine life, and distinctive underwater vistas.

The underwater world of Oman is breathtaking, particularly at well-known dive locations like the Daymaniyat Islands, Musandam Peninsula, and Hallaniyat Islands. There are numerous diving sites available at the Daymaniyat Islands, a protected natural reserve, for both novice and expert divers. Divers can see a variety of marine life in the clear waters, including turtles, rays, and schools of vivid fish that dart around the brilliant coral formations. Due to its magnificent fjords, the Musandam Peninsula is regarded as the "Norway of Arabia" and offers divers an incredible setting against which to explore breathtaking underwater cliffs and come in contact with dolphins and whale sharks.

In Oman, snorkeling is equally interesting, and several spots are reachable from the coast. Snorkelers love to visit Bander Khayran, a lovely harbor close to Muscat, where the waters are pristine and filled with marine life. Another snorkeling haven is Salalah's stunning beaches, which are located in Dhofar's southern district. Here, you may swim with a variety of tropical fish and bright coral reefs.

Meeting the docile and amiable whale sharks that inhabit the seas off the shore is one of the joys of diving and snorkeling in Oman. As the largest fish in the world, these spectacular beings provide divers and snorkelers with a once-in-a-lifetime opportunity to swim alongside them in their natural environment.

It is admirable that Oman is so committed to protecting its marine environment. The government has made enormous efforts to safeguard the coastal ecosystems, making sure they are preserved in their natural state and continue to flourish for many years to come. This dedication is demonstrated by the creation of marine protected areas and stringent guidelines for diving and fishing operations.

Oman's crystal-clear waters call you to discover their undiscovered wonders whether you're an experienced diver or just a curious snorkeler. The nation's unrivaled destination for diving and snorkeling excursions, abundant marine biodiversity, and dedication to conservation leave visitors with priceless memories of a lifetime spent underwater.

8.2 Trekking And Hiking In The Mountains

A spectacular journey, trekking and hiking in Oman's mountains reveals the nation's breathtaking natural beauty and untamed terrain. The Arabian Peninsula's southernmost country, Oman, has a varied geography, and its mountains provide some of the most alluring trekking opportunities in the world.

The picturesque Al Hajar Mountains, which span along Oman's northern shore, are one of the most well-liked places for trekking. The renowned Jebel Shams, often known as the "Mountain of the Sun," is located within the Al Hajar Mountains. As Oman's highest point, this majestic summit offers adventurous hikers breath-taking views of the vast Wadi Ghul (Oman's Grand Canyon) and the surrounding scenery.

The scenic Jebel Akhdar, often known as "Green Mountain," is a must-see for anyone looking for a more leisurely climb. This lush mountain is renowned for its terraced fruit orchards, historic towns, and cool environment, making it the perfect summertime getaway.

The wadis (dry riverbeds) that are abundant in Oman's hilly landscape are excellent for hiking. A well-liked option is Wadi Bani Khalid, which has emerald green ponds surrounded by rocky cliffs, providing an oasis-like atmosphere. Another well-known location is Wadi Shab, which is well-known for its lush greenery, caverns, and crystal-clear waters that tempt hikers to explore more.

The ascent of the "Green Mountain," or Jabal al Akdhar, is one of Oman's most distinctive mountain experiences. Adventurers can experience the traditional way of life in the mountains as well as traditional Omani communities and old terraced fields on this strenuous walk.

Safety is of the utmost importance in Oman's highlands, as it is on any trekking or climbing excursion. Being prepared is essential, as is dressing appropriately, wearing the proper footwear, and having enough water and food on hand. Although some trails can be accessed without a tour, using a local guide can improve the experience and offer insights into the history, culture, and natural beauties of the area.

Trekking and climbing in Oman's highlands provide a chance to get in touch with nature, take in breath-taking views, and fully immerse oneself in the area's rich cultural legacy. The mountains of Oman offer a memorable journey for outdoor enthusiasts and nature lovers, whether ascending difficult peaks or discovering tranquil valleys.

8.3 Dolphin Watching And Coastal Excursions

Visitors may see the grace and majesty of these mighty marine creatures in their natural habitat while enjoying dolphin watching and seaside excursions in Oman. Oman is a top location for dolphin aficionados and environment lovers since its coastal waters are home to a variety of dolphin species, such as lively bottlenose dolphins, acrobatic spinner dolphins, and beautiful humpback dolphins.

The capital of Oman, Muscat, is one of the most well-liked places to see dolphins. Numerous tour companies provide guided trips into the Arabian Sea's deep blue seas, where dolphin pods are frequently seen playing and swimming next to the boats. Visitors of all ages are captivated by the sight of these sociable and clever animals leaping and diving in the clear waters, and the experience leaves a lasting effect.

Beyond dolphin viewing, Oman's coastal excursions provide visitors the chance to explore the country's stunning coastline, which is filled with undiscovered coves, white sand beaches, and craggy cliffs. A lot of trips stop at isolated locations, letting travelers enjoy swimming, snorkeling, and even picnics while taking in the quiet splendor of the Omani coastline.

The ability to see other marine life, including sea turtles, rays, and a variety of colorful fish that live on coral reefs, is another perk of taking coastal trips. The dedication of Oman to marine conservation guarantees the preservation of these coastal ecosystems' purity and biodiversity.

In Oman, the months of October through April are often the greatest for coastal trips and dolphin viewing because of the pleasant weather and quiet waters. Local tour operators and guides are knowledgeable about dolphin behavior and the best places to watch them, offering a responsible and sustainable experience for both people and marine life.

The coastal tours provide insights into Oman's nautical history and the traditional fishing towns that are still thriving along the coast in addition to the spectacular natural beauty. The experience is enhanced by interacting with the locals' culture and learning about their close ties to the sea.

To sum up, Oman's coastal excursions and dolphin watching offer a delightful fusion of natural beauty, marine variety, and cultural experiences. Oman's coastal waters offer a unique trip that will leave you with treasured memories of this intriguing Arabian Peninsula gem, whether you are a wildlife fanatic, a nature lover, or simply seeking a calm and soul-soothing experience.

8.4 Off-Road Adventures And Camping In The Wilderness

Exploring the country's untamed and rocky landscapes is made exciting and immersive by off-road excursions and camping in Oman's wilderness. Outdoor lovers and off-road enthusiasts alike are drawn to Oman by its varied environment, which includes enormous deserts, soaring dunes, steep mountains, and isolated wadis.

The Wahiba Sands, a vast desert that runs for hundreds of kilometers, is one of Oman's most well-known off-road locations. Dune bashing, an exhilarating pastime where 4x4 vehicles go up and down the dunes' steep slopes, is made possible by this enormous expanse of golden sand dunes. A genuine connection to the wilderness is made possible by the exciting and humble feeling of flying across the shifting dunes.

It is very lovely to camp in the Omani bush. The sky becomes a painting of vivid colors as the sun sets over the desert, providing a fantastic backdrop for stargazing. You can escape the modern world and savor the quiet of nature by setting up camp among the dunes or near a peaceful wadi. Camping in Oman is a special chance to experience Bedouin hospitality because some trips provide guests the option to camp in authentic Bedouin tents and enjoy delicious local cuisine and friendly Arabian hospitality.

Along with the desert, Oman's untamed mountains provide fantastic chances for off-roading and camping. Off-road enthusiasts will find the Hajar Mountains' majestic peaks and historic settlements to be both demanding and rewarding. One can see the traditional Omani way of life and the resiliency of its inhabitants in the face of the tough climate by exploring the isolated villages and secret valleys.

Another off-road marvel is Oman's wadis, which offer an oasis of life despite the desert surroundings. Adventurers can find secret lakes, waterfalls, and lush foliage that thrive in these remote areas of the forest by driving across stony wadi beds and via winding trails.

Off-roading in Oman requires extreme caution, so it's essential to have the right gear, a well-kept vehicle, and a trustworthy GPS system. Many adventurers decide to sign up for guided tours run by knowledgeable locals who are familiar with the area and can guarantee a secure and educational experience.

In conclusion, Oman's off-road excursions and wild camping provide an enthralling escape into a world of natural marvels and cultural legacy. Oman's untamed landscapes entice daring spirits to embrace the thrill of the great outdoors and create priceless experiences in the center of the Arabian Peninsula, whether it be dune bashing in the desert, trekking rough mountains, or finding hidden wadis.

CHAPTER NINE

Traditional Arts And Crafts

9.1 Omani Handicrafts And Souvenirs

Oman, a country with a rich history and traditions, is well known for its exquisite handicrafts and mementos. Through the decades, these ancient arts have been passed down, representing the history, culture, and way of life of the nation. Omani handicrafts and souvenirs are more than just something to buy; they represent the spirit of the nation and are treasured by both residents and visitors.

Silverware is one of the most well-known Omani crafts. Jewelry, daggers (khanjars), and home decor are just a few examples of the objects that showcase the exquisite designs and skilled craftsmanship of silver artists. The traditional motifs used in each artwork, such as the

Omani khanjar, which stands for bravery and hospitality, each convey a different tale.

Pottery making is a respected skill that is strongly ingrained in Oman's culture. Vases, plates, and incense burners are just a few of the items that skilled potters produce using age-old methods that have been handed down through the generations. The country's distinctive architecture and the natural world serve as inspiration for the pottery's frequent use of vivid colors and intricate designs.

The country's artisanal heritage also holds a unique place for Omani textiles. Using handlooms, the ancient technique of weaving creates exquisite clothing, rugs, and tapestries. The ornate Omani kumma, a distinctive cap that is an integral feature of the nation's traditional male clothing, is the most well-known Omani textile.

Another form of art that displays the extraordinary skills of Omani craftsmen is woodwork. They make exquisitely crafted furniture, doors, and decorative things out of local woods like rosewood and teak. The patterns frequently combine geometric shapes, floral themes, and Quranic passages, illustrating how culture and religion can coexist.

Traditional incense burners (mabkharahs), Khanjar reproductions, and hand-made Omani perfumes are popular choices for tourists looking to bring home a bit of Omani culture. In Oman, frankincense and myrrh from the Dhofar region are prized souvenirs because of their enormous cultural and historical significance.

In addition to being works of art, Omani handicrafts and souvenirs are important drivers of the regional economy. For the preservation of the nation's cultural history and to give craftsmen a means of supporting themselves, the Omani government and numerous organizations actively encourage and promote these crafts.

9.2 Oud Making And Perfume Blending

Oman, a country rich in history and olfactory delights, has a long history of producing oud and combining perfumes. The highly esteemed and sought-after fragrance oud, commonly referred to as "liquid gold," is made from the resinous heartwood of the Aquilaria tree. Omani culture is strongly rooted in the skillful extraction of oud and the art of perfume combining, which combine history, craftsmanship, and aromatic pleasure.

The Aquilaria tree, which is native to certain areas of Oman, is first infected with a particular kind of mold as the first step in the production of oud. The creation of the valuable resin, which gives oud its alluring aroma, is sparked by this illness. The trees are harvested and the resinous heartwood is collected after a number of years, once the resin has adequately matured. The production of Oud oil from this resin requires excellent distillation, which takes time and knowledge.

The woody, balsamic, and sweet elements of the oud oil produced by Oman's aquilaria trees are what give it its distinctive and alluring scent. It is one of the most prized types in the world and is greatly coveted by perfumers and fans of fragrance everywhere.

Along with Oud, Oman is renowned for its long-standing practice of scent blending. The technique of perfume blending includes expertly fusing diverse natural perfumes and essential oils to produce distinctive and alluring scents. These scents, referred to as "Ittars," are an essential component of Omani culture and are used for a variety of rituals and ceremonies, including personal decoration and religious events.

In order to create a harmonious and seductive aroma, the process of perfume mixing entails choosing premium natural ingredients like rose, jasmine, sandalwood, and saffron and carefully blending them in specific quantities. In order to create magnificent and evocative aromas that capture the essence of Oman's varied landscapes and cultural heritage, perfume blenders, or "Attars," employ their great sense of smell and in-depth expertise.

The traditions of combining perfume and manufacturing in Oman are more than simply businesses; they stand for a cultural legacy that has been conserved and passed down through the generations. These aromatic gems continue to be vital to Oman's economy and sense of cultural identity, luring travelers and lovers from all over the world to take in the alluring scents of this stunning and unique region.

9.3 The Art Of Silver And Gold Jewelry

The creation of silver and gold jewelry is a deeply ingrained part of the Sultanate of Oman's rich cultural history. The history, traditions, and artistic prowess of the Omani people are reflected in the elaborate and intriguing jewelry that Omani artists have been making for generations. The jewelry has great cultural and social significance since it represents money, status, and ties to the family.

The art of crafting silver and gold jewelry in Oman calls for extraordinary dexterity and accuracy. The exquisite finishing and elaborate designs of Omani artists' works are clear indications of their skill. The jewelry is decorated with traditional designs that are drawn from nature, Islamic geometric patterns, and historical symbols, giving each piece a special and significant quality.

Oman places a high value on silver jewelry and considers it an integral element of its culture. Omani women frequently wear silver jewelry, which has sentimental meaning because it is handed down from one generation to the next. The silver jewelry includes anklets, rings, earrings, bracelets, and necklaces with elaborate designs. The Khanjar pendant, which is a portrayal of the traditional Omani dagger and has significant historical and cultural value, is one of the most recognizable items of Omani silver jewelry.

Additionally, gold jewelry has a unique position in Omani culture, especially at festive occasions like weddings. The exquisite patterns, which frequently use precious stones like sapphires, emeralds, and rubies, add to the jewelry's charm. The matching necklaces, earrings, and bracelets seen in traditional Omani gold jewelry sets are what give them their beauty.

In Oman, the craft of creating silver and gold jewelry is not just practiced in for-profit establishments; it is also a thriving cottage industry. Jewelry making is a long-standing tradition in many rural areas, with knowledge being passed down from one generation to the next. These craftsmen are actively supported by the government and numerous cultural institutions in maintaining their craft and history.

The bustling souks (markets) of Oman are a treasure mine of silver and gold jewelry for travellers. Visitors can explore the stunning displays of classic and modern designs and immerse themselves in the rich history and artistic excellence. The jewelry serves as both a lovely memento and a physical reflection of the nation's artistic and cultural heritage.

In conclusion, Oman's tradition of producing fine silver and gold jewelry is a monument to the country's artistic prowess and sense of cultural pride. Every item has a narrative that represents social values, traditions, and customs of the Omani people. These stunning jewelry pieces continue to amaze and inspire people whether they are worn as personal adornments or treasured as family heirlooms, contributing significantly to Oman's enduring history of beauty and craftsmanship.

CHAPTER TEN

Festivals And Celebrations

10.1 Muscat Festival And Other Cultural Events

The Arabian Peninsula's southeast coast nation of Oman is recognized for its vibrant customs and rich cultural history. The Muscat Festival is the most well-known of the many cultural celebrations of Oman's history, arts, music, and folklore that are held throughout the year. The Omani people's dedication to preserving and promoting their cultural identity is demonstrated by this yearly event.

The month-long Muscat Festival typically takes place in January or February and draws both locals and visitors. The celebration is held throughout the nation, including the capital city of Muscat. Its main goal is to highlight Oman's rich cultural heritage through a variety of artistic performances, handicrafts, music, dance, and delectable cuisine.

Visitors can immerse themselves in a busy cultural village that replicates the traditional Omani way of life at the festival's center. Intricate pottery, silverware, textiles, and other traditional handicrafts are proudly displayed here by artisans and craftsmen. Visitors can participate in workshops to pick up these abilities, preserving Omani craftsmanship.

The Muscat Festival includes music and dance acts that mix contemporary music with traditional Omani melodies. Local musicians enchant the gathering with their melodic "oud" and "rebaba" sounds as folkloric troupes from several regions perform energizing dances like the "Razha" and "Liwa."

Foodies are treated to a feast of traditional and delectable Omani foods. Visitors can savor delectable foods like "shuwa" (slow-cooked marinated lamb) and "halwa" (a sweet, sticky confection made from dates, ghee, and sugar) at food vendors. The essence of hospitality and kindness is demonstrated through this culinary experience, which is a fundamental component of Omani culture.

Oman also organizes various cultural events all year long in addition to the Muscat Festival. One such occasion is the Salalah Tourism Festival, which takes place in the southern district of Dhofar throughout the summer. During the Khareef season, when the region transforms into lush green landscapes that stand in stark contrast to the dry deserts of the rest of the nation, this celebration is held. Traditional performances, folklore exhibits, and heritage performances are all part of the Salalah Tourism Festival.

The National Day celebrations on November 18th, which honor Oman's independence and Sultan Qaboos bin Said al Said's birthday, are among the other noteworthy occasions. Parades, fireworks, and a variety of cultural acts are all part of these celebrations, which promote a sense of patriotism and unity throughout the country.

In conclusion, Oman's cultural celebrations, particularly the Muscat Festival, offer residents and guests a singular chance to immerse themselves in the nation's rich legacy. The Omani people's commitment to upholding their traditions and practices while embracing modernization and inclusivity is demonstrated by these events. One may genuinely understand the friendliness, generosity, and ingrained cultural values of the Omanis by taking part in various cultural events.

10.2 Ramadan Traditions And Eid Festivities

The holy month of Ramadan, during which Muslims fast, is a crucial period for Muslims in Oman and all throughout the world. Omanis observe a number of customs and rituals throughout this holy month in order to develop their spirituality and strengthen their ties to their religion. The joyful Eid celebrations that mark the end of Ramadan also unite the neighborhood in a sense of solidarity and appreciation.

Ramadan customs: In Oman, Ramadan is marked by a spirit of piety and devotion. An essential component of the holy month is the 24-hour fast. Omanis get up early for "suhoor," a pre-dawn meal, to eat and prepare for the upcoming day of fasting. Families assemble for "iftar," the breaking of the fast, when the sun begins to set. The Prophet Muhammad (PBUH) set an example by breaking his fast with dates and water.

During Ramadan, mosques all around the nation come alive with special nighttime prayers called "Taraweeh." Muslims have the chance to recite and listen to the Qur'an during these prolonged prayers, contemplating on its messages and seeking spiritual enlightenment.

Omani Ramadan traditions place a strong emphasis on donating and charity. It is a season when people and organizations are more likely to show kindness and generosity by giving food, money, and other forms of support to those who are in need. As communities come together to make sure that everyone may experience the blessings of Ramadan, there is a tangible sense of understanding and compassion.

Celebrations for Eid: In Oman, Eid al-Fitr, the celebration of breaking the fast, is a significant event because it signifies the conclusion of Ramadan. Muslims assemble in mosques and public spaces for a special Eid prayer to express their appreciation to Allah for guiding them during the month-long fast.

Families in Omani dress to the nines and give youngsters "Eidiyah," money presents given by elders as a sign of blessings and love. Families frequently visit friends and family to exchange warm greetings and indulge in mouthwatering regional cuisine. During Eid, feasts with delectable delicacies like "maqbous" (spiced rice with meat) and "halwa" (sweet dessert) take center stage.

In Oman, Eid is a time of joy and celebration. Throughout the nation, many cultural activities, musical performances, and traditional dances are held. The capital city of Muscat transforms into a center of festivities, drawing both locals and visitors. The night sky is illuminated by fireworks, giving the celebrations a magical touch.

10.3 National Day Celebrations

Every year on November 18, the Omani people commemorate their National Day, a major day with great significance to them. On this day, Oman celebrates its independence and remembers the revered late Sultan Qaboos bin Said al Said, who was instrumental in reshaping the country and guiding it toward development and prosperity. The National Day celebrations are evidence of the Omani people's profound pride in their illustrious past, distinctive culture, and remarkable achievements.

The celebrations, which start a few days before November 18th and last for a week, instill joy and a sense of solidarity among all Americans. The Omani flag and colorful decorative lights are placed on buildings and streets to represent the sense of patriotism and national pride.

The capital city of Muscat, where a large parade is held, is where the celebrations' epicenter is located. The parade displays the discipline and commitment to the country of the Omani Armed Forces, Royal Oman

Police, and other government agencies. The audience are enthralled as vibrant floats portraying many facets of Omani culture, tradition, and accomplishments go through the streets.

Performances of traditional music and dancing give the event a festive atmosphere. The lively "Razha" and "Liwa" dances performed by folkloric troupes, accompanied by the rhythmic beats of traditional instruments, add to the festive atmosphere of the celebrations.

The entire city is illuminated by the magnificent display that fireworks produce in the night sky. The flashes of colors and patterns stand for Oman's future wealth and hope.

The National Day celebrations also include a variety of cultural activities and displays that highlight Omani tradition, artwork, and food. Both tourists and residents can enjoy the distinctive flavors of the country by viewing the beautiful handicrafts on show and traditional Omani cuisine being provided.

The sense of community throughout this festive week is further strengthened by family get-togethers and neighborhood activities. Warm greetings are given, historical tales are spoken, and people reaffirm their dedication to the advancement and prosperity of their country.

CHAPTER ELEVEN

Responsible Travel And Sustainability

11.1 Supporting Local Communities

In order to promote sustainable economic growth, protect cultural assets, and ensure social cohesion, local communities must be supported. The Sultanate of Oman focuses a lot of emphasis on community development because of its varied landscapes and rich cultural tapestry. Various programs and tactics have been put into place nationwide to strengthen and empower local communities.

Economic empowerment is one of the main ways Oman helps its local communities. The government promotes entrepreneurship and the growth of small businesses by offering funding and incentives. Through numerous domestic and international markets and fairs, local artisans and craftsmen are given the chance to display their traditional abilities and goods. This helps maintain traditional arts and crafts that are strongly ingrained in Omani culture while also boosting the local economy.

Supporting local communities also places a high priority on education and skill development. To ensure that everyone has access to a high-quality education, the government funds the construction of schools, colleges, and facilities for vocational training in rural areas. Oman trains its communities to engage in the contemporary labor market and contribute to the general growth of the country by providing the local populace with necessary skills.

Supporting local communities also means protecting cultural treasures. By establishing museums, cultural centers, and heritage locations, Oman's unique cultural character is preserved. With pride, locals observe traditional events, festivals, and ceremonies, which promote a sense of community among residents and draw tourists, boosting the local economy.

The government is concentrating on establishing medical facilities in outlying areas, although healthcare is not neglected. The local population's wellbeing and the creation of a healthier workforce, both of which are necessary for economic growth, are ensured by access to inexpensive, high-quality healthcare services.

Oman also encourages eco-friendly behaviors and sustainable tourism, ensuring that the nation's natural beauty is preserved. The environment is preserved for future generations while local communities gain from more job opportunities thanks to the promotion of responsible tourism.

11.2 Eco-Friendly Practices In Oman

Oman has been actively encouraging environmentally friendly behaviors and emphasizing the value of environmental preservation and sustainable development. Through a number of projects and policies, the nation has demonstrated its dedication to protecting its natural resources and minimizing its ecological impact.

Renewable energy is one of the main areas in Oman where eco-friendly techniques are highlighted. The nation has made significant investments in renewable energy initiatives, particularly in wind and solar energy. Large-scale wind and solar farms have been put in place, utilizing the plentiful natural resources to provide clean energy. These initiatives not only lower greenhouse gas emissions, but also open the door to a future that is greener and uses less energy.

Another important area of eco-friendly measures in Oman is water conservation. Given its dry climate, water is a limited resource that requires careful management. Drip irrigation in agriculture and water recycling systems in urban areas are only two examples of the water-saving initiatives the government has put in place. Additionally, public awareness efforts encourage the community to use water responsibly.

Oman is committed to protecting its natural environments and biodiversity. To conserve endangered species and their habitats, a number of protected areas have been established, including the Ras al-Jinz Turtle Reserve and the Arabian Oryx Sanctuary. Additionally, current programs to reforest and afforest areas to fight desertification are helping to save soil and sequester carbon.

Recycling and waste management are aggressively encouraged to reduce their negative effects on the environment. In order to promote acceptable waste disposal practices among its people and businesses, Oman has put in place trash separation and recycling programs. Additionally, efforts are undertaken to limit single-use plastics through the prohibition of some plastic products and the promotion of environmentally suitable alternatives.

Another essential component of Oman's eco-friendly activities is sustainable tourism. The nation is renowned for its breathtaking landscapes and rich cultural legacy, and efforts are made to manage tourism in an environmentally responsible way. Visitors are educated about respecting nature and local communities, and tour operators and businesses are urged to use sustainable practices.

11.3 Respecting Oman's Wildlife And Nature

It is crucial to respect Oman's wildlife and natural surroundings because the nation is endowed with a variety of ecosystems, a rich biodiversity, and distinctive natural landscapes. To secure the preservation of these priceless resources for future generations, it is crucial to adopt a conservation-minded strategy.

Responsible tourism is one of the main strategies to respect Oman's wildlife and natural environment. When exploring natural regions, visitors are urged to act ethically by keeping on authorized trails, respecting wildlife, and not leaving any rubbish behind. Wadis, deserts, and marine reserves are just a few of Oman's natural attractions that draw lots of visitors, and responsible tourism makes sure that these places are preserved and fun for everyone.

To protect its distinctive flora and fauna, the Sultanate has created a number of protected areas and wildlife reserves. This contains the famed Arabian Oryx Sanctuary, where it is preserved and thriving after formerly being on the verge of extinction. These protected areas are essential for maintaining rare and endangered animals as well as their natural ecosystems.

Furthermore, Oman's initiatives to stop wildlife trafficking show its dedication to protecting the natural world. With a zero-tolerance policy toward poaching and smuggling, the nation has strict rules and regulations in place to combat the illegal trade in wildlife and its products.

Adopting sustainable methods in fishing, agriculture, and other sectors of the economy that interact with the environment is another way to respect Oman's animals and natural resources. To lessen the impact on ecosystems, the government promotes the use of environmentally friendly farming practices such organic farming and irrigation that uses less water. The long-term sustainability of marine resources is also supported by the promotion of sustainable fishing methods.

The population of Oman is being encouraged to respect nature and wildlife through public awareness campaigns and educational initiatives. Learning about the value of conservation and their part in preserving the environment is a priority in schools and communities. These programs seek to instil in residents a sense of ownership and accountability that will motivate them to actively engage in conservation efforts.

Final Thought

After an amazing tour through the pages of the Oman travel guide, you can't help but be in awe of the alluring attractions that this Middle Eastern treasure has to offer. Oman, a nation that radiates an alluring fusion of age-old customs and cutting-edge wonders, is a visitor's paradise that captures the heart and soul of every intrepid tourist who steps foot on its magnificent grounds.

The guidebook has revealed Oman's genuine spirit with every page turn—a nation of contrasts where centuries-old traditions coexist peacefully with a forward-looking outlook on the future. Travelers from all over the world are drawn to it by its rich culture, friendly people, and breathtaking surroundings.

You have been taken on a fascinating journey through time by the handbook as it has led you through Oman's historic treasures. The historic forts, such Nizwa Fort and Bahla Fort, have proudly stood as silent witnesses to the heroic tales and rich history of Oman. Travelers are in awe of the architectural wonders that serve as a witness to Oman's illustrious history as a result of their towering walls protecting the nation's heritage.

The travel guide's description of Oman's natural splendor has permanently imprinted your soul. Oman's landscapes are a work of art, painted with vibrant colors and various ecosystems, and they range from the immaculate beaches along the azure Arabian Sea to the towering mountains of Jebel Akhdar and the breathtaking deserts of Wahiba Sands. You have found a calm oasis that provides relief from the bustle of contemporary life while exploring the rocky wadis and lush oases.

You have been drawn in by the charm of Muscat, the nation's capital, as you have read the guidebook's suggestions for must-see locations. Muscat's large mosques, notably the Sultan Qaboos large Mosque, and its busy souks, where the perfume of frankincense blends with that of exotic spices, are clear examples of the city's fusion of old-world beauty and modern elegance. The elegantly sailing traditional dhows in the port convey tales of Oman's nautical heritage, while the contemporary skyscrapers show the country's hopes for development.

You have been introduced to Omani hospitality, which is known for its warmth and friendliness. You have been treated with sincere smiles and warm welcomes by the locals, who have encouraged you to take part in their traditions and celebrations. Traditional Omani food has been a gourmet joy, leaving you wanting more after tasting its delicious flavors of spices and rich fragrances.

You won't soon forget the sensation of adventure the handbook sparked in you, luring you to discover Oman's off-the-beaten-path locations. You have found refuge in Oman's untamed wilderness by exploring the mysterious valleys, setting up camp beneath the stars, and finding prehistoric petroglyphs carved into the rocks.

Beyond the fascinating topography and cultural encounters, the handbook also discusses Oman's proud conservation initiatives. You have been inspired by the nation's commitment to safeguarding its distinctive species, including the endangered Arabian Oryx, as a responsible traveler.

The travel guide to Oman's last chapters make you yearn to set out on this unforgettable journey. Its ineffable moments of self-discovery and connection with a place that has seen the passage of time are what give Oman its charm in addition to its tangible wonders. Oman offers an experience unlike any other, whether you're a daring adventurer, a history buff, or a peace-seeker.

You are utterly indebted to this travel guide for the vivid insights it has given you as you appreciate your final reflections on it. You have been forever changed by the differences of Oman, and you can't wait to experience its enigmatic allure. You are now prepared to embark on a once-in-a-lifetime vacation, anxious to explore the attraction of Oman, using the handbook as your compass.

SAFE TRAVEL!

Printed in Great Britain
by Amazon

38555863R00066